Valley Forge

by RICHARD AMMON

illustrated by
BILL FARNSWORTH

HOLIDAY HOUSE / New York

to Cari and Elizabeth
R. A.

to R. A. from B. F.

Library of Congress Cataloging-in-Publication Data
Ammon, Richard
Valley Forge / by Richard Ammon; illustrated by Bill Farnsworth—1st ed.
p. cm.
Includes bibliographical references.
ISBN 0-8234-1746-8 (hardcover)
ISBN 0-8234-2016-7 (paperback)
1. Washington, George, 1732–1799—Headquarters—Pennsylvania—Valley Forge—Juvenile literature.
2. Valley Forge (Pa.)—History—18th century—Juvenile literature. 3. United States. Continental Army—Military life—Juvenile literature.
4. United States—History—Revolution, 1775–1783—Juvenile literature.
[1. United States—History—Revolution, 1775–1783—Campaigns.
2. Valley Forge (Pa.) 3. United States. Continental Army—Military life.]
I. Farnsworth, Bill, ill. II Title.
E234.A46 2004
973.3'341—dc22   2003068569

ISBN-13: 978-0-8234-1746-9 (hardcover)   ISBN-10: 0-8234-1746-8 (hardcover)
ISBN-13: 978-0-8234-2016-2 (paperback)   ISBN-10: 0-8234-2016-7 (paperback)

AUTHOR'S NOTE

Russell Freedman once said, "What every historian and biographer dreads [is] to be waylaid by the slippery nature of facts, to be mugged by the elusiveness of truth, to get all the facts right and still be wrong!" That remark couldn't apply more to the story of Valley Forge, a saga wrapped in myth and legend.

This book would not have been possible without the expert advice of Lee Boyle, historian for the National Park Service at Valley Forge. Not only did he direct me to the appropriate sources, but he also was able to point out those stories found in various sources that are unsupported by primary sources. For example, he pointed out that much written about Martha Washington is "romantic drivel."

Boyle has also kept me current with revisionist history. Growing up in Ephrata, Pennsylvania, I had learned that the wounded from Brandywine had been taken to the Ephrata Cloister, a religious community. However, recent research suggests that these wounded and sick soldiers were not taken to Ephrata until mid-December, about the time the Continental army camped at Valley Forge.

Great effort was taken to tell the story of Valley Forge as accurately as possible. Of course, there are volumes of books and materials on Valley Forge. In trying to make this book accessible for children, it was my job to include what I thought was relevant and to eliminate all sorts of fascinating information, such as the constantly changing numbers of men assigned to Valley Forge, records of supplies, and letter upon letter from Washington to the Continental Congress requesting materials and supplies. Aaron Burr was at Valley Forge, but to explain him more than to say he killed Alexander Hamilton, I felt, detracted from this telling.

SEEDS OF WAR

Long before the Revolutionary War began, George Washington and other Americans worried that England was taking away certain freedoms. The British passed laws taxing the citizens of the thirteen colonies without giving them representatives in Parliament. On the night of December 16, 1773, citizens dressed up like Native Americans and dumped chests of tea from English ships into Boston Harbor to protest the tax on tea. This protest has been forever known as the Boston Tea Party.

Americans continued to speak out against this taxation without representation. In Virginia on March 23, 1775, Patrick Henry delivered his famous speech, ending with "Give me Liberty or Give me Death!" Yet the last thing most people in America wanted was to break away from Great Britain.

Many changed their minds on April 18, 1775, when British General Thomas Gage ordered his troops to capture guns and ammunition that the patriots had stored at Concord, Massachusetts. Paul Revere, William Dawes, and Dr. Samuel Prescott rode ahead to warn their fellow countrymen that the British were coming. No one knows for sure what happened early the next morning, April 19, when seventy minutemen faced six hundred British soldiers. Some say the British fired first. Others believe that a retreating patriot may have tripped over his own gun, and it went off. No matter how it started, when the fight was over, eight minutemen lay dead. By the time the British returned to Boston, patriots attacked them from all sides, killing or wounding nearly half of them. The war few people wanted had begun.

In towns and villages throughout the colonies, groups of men formed local militia units. From the outskirts of Boston, thousands of armed New Englanders tormented the British. Since the thirteen colonies were not yet a nation, there was no united regular army. So, representatives in the Continental Congress meeting in Philadelphia decided the time had come to take action.

On June 14, 1775, John Adams urged the Continental Congress to appoint George Washington commander in chief of the army. In the French and Indian Wars, Washington had led the Virginia army for the British. Unfortunately, he knew little about making military plans, he had no experience with directing artillery, and he had never commanded a large army. Still, most representatives believed that Washington was the right man for the job because he had the leadership qualities people admired. He was patient, determined, and always polite.

He also possessed charisma and charm. Standing six feet two inches tall, Washington towered over most of his officers. With blue eyes and brown hair powdered white, he was good-looking and majestic, especially in his blue army uniform. When Washington entered a room, eyes turned toward him. His stepgrandson, George Custis, said, "He rode [his horse] as he did everything, with ease, elegance, and with power."

TIME LINE

December 16, 1773	Boston Tea Party
March 23, 1775	Patrick Henry delivers his famous speech, "Give me Liberty or Give me Death!"
April 18, 1775	Revere, Dawes, and Prescott ride to warn citizens that the British are coming.
April 19, 1775	Battles of Lexington and Concord
June 14, 1775	George Washington is appointed commander in chief.
July 4, 1776	Declaration of Independence is signed.
December 26, 1776	Washington surprises the Hessians at Trenton, New Jersey.
September 11, 1777	British defeat Washington along Brandywine Creek at Chadds Ford, Pennsylvania.
September 26, 1777	British enter Philadelphia.
October 4, 1777	British defeat Washington at Germantown, Pennsylvania.
October 14–November 15	Americans defend Fort Mercer.
October 17, 1777	British surrender to Horatio Gates at Saratoga, New York.
October 22, 1777	Americans defend Fort Mercer.
November 16, 1777	Americans abandon Fort Mifflin.
November 21, 1777	Americans abandon Fort Mercer.
December 19, 1777	Washington camps at Valley Forge. Stormy winds and piercing cold. Temperature: 30°F
December 1777	Washington orders soldiers to build huts. The last huts are completed in February.
December 25, 1777	Snows four inches
December 30, 1777	Temperature: 6°F
January 1778	Lowest temperature in January: 12°F
February 6, 1778	France signs alliance with the Americans.
February 8, 1778	A "deep" snow
February 9–10, 1778	Heavy rains
February 10, 1778	Martha Washington arrives in camp.
February 1778	Baron von Steuben arrives in camp. Lowest temperature in February: 16°F
March 2–3, 1778	Enough snow for sledding. Lowest temperature in March: 8°F
March 9–10, 1778	Winter begins to break.
March 17, 1778	St. Patrick's Day
May 6, 1778	Word finally reaches Valley Forge that France will help the Continentals. The entire camp celebrates.
June 18, 1778	Washington breaks camp at Valley Forge.
June 28, 1778	Battle of Monmouth, New Jersey
1779–1781	War shifts to battles in North and South Carolina and Georgia.
October 19, 1781	British General Cornwallis surrenders to Washington at Yorktown, Virginia.

SEPTEMBER 1777: PRELUDE TO VALLEY FORGE

When Washington took command of the Continental army, it was made up mostly of ordinary citizens. These New England militia were neither well equipped nor well trained, and they looked nothing like the professional British soldiers.

For most of the first two years the Americans won few battles, but this ragtag army still gave the redcoats trouble. The British government decided to end this rebellion once and for all. They planned a campaign for the summer of 1777 to split the colonies in two. British General John Burgoyne marched south from Canada along Lake Champlain, intending to reach the Hudson River and to capture New York State.

At the same time, British General William Howe set sail from New York for Chesapeake Bay. From the northern point of the bay, Howe began marching toward Philadelphia. Washington rushed his men to block Howe's soldiers.

On September 11, 1777, the Americans met the British along Brandywine Creek at Chadds Ford, Pennsylvania. There the two armies fought a fierce battle. Eventually, the British outmaneuvered the patriots. The Americans retreated to avoid being trapped.

With the path clear, the British entered Philadelphia on September 26, 1777. Had this war been fought in Europe, it probably would have been over as soon as the British had taken the American capital. But this wasn't Europe. America was not much more than thirteen states united to fight for their freedom. The Continental Congress fled to York, Pennsylvania, where the delegates continued their work until the summer of 1778.

Washington's Rules of Civility

Washington always believed in fairness. When he was fourteen years old, he wrote 110 "Rules of Civility," or rules to live by. The twelfth rule said: "Shake not the head, feet or legs; roll not the eyes; lift not one eyebrow higher than the other."

The forty-seventh said: "Mock not nor jest at any thing of importance; break no jests that are sharp biting," which means that you should not make fun of important things, or tell mean jokes.

The eighty-ninth said: "Speak not evil of the absent, for it is unjust." This rule means you shouldn't talk behind someone's back because it's not fair to that person.

OCTOBER AND NOVEMBER 1777

After General Howe took Philadelphia, his army set up camp north of the city in Germantown. At Trenton, New Jersey, on the morning after Christmas 1776, Washington had surprised a group of Hessians, German soldiers fighting for the British. He hoped to repeat his success on October fourth and catch the British unprepared in Germantown. Unfortunately, it was foggy on the morning of the Battle of Germantown. When the fog mixed with smoke from firing muskets, soldiers could not see more than a few yards. Americans fired at one another, and the attack was a failure.

Even with the defeats at Brandywine and Germantown, Washington and his troops did not lose hope. The British also realized that ending the rebellion was not going to be as easy as they had expected. General Burgoyne surrendered to American General Horatio Gates on October 17, 1777, after the Battles of Saratoga.

Following the Battle of Germantown, Washington marched his army northwest of Philadelphia. From there he directed the defense of two forts: Fort Mercer, along the Delaware River at Red Bank, New Jersey, and Fort Mifflin, on an island in the Delaware River.

On October 22, 1777, Americans held Fort Mercer against an attack by the Hessians, but they had to abandon the fort on November 21 when General Charles Cornwallis approached with a large force. For several weeks the British bombarded Fort Mifflin until the Americans had no choice but to leave on November 16.

Marquis de Lafayette

Lafayette was born in France on September 6, 1757. When he was nineteen, he set sail for America to join the Revolution. Soon after he landed Lafayette wrote to the president of Congess, John Hancock, volunteering to fight without pay. On July 31, 1777, Congress conferred upon Lafayette the rank of major general. Since Washington needed all the help he could get, he welcomed Lafayette into the Continental army.

Washington wasn't sure how he could use this very young French major general, but at the Battle of Brandywine, Lafayette not only distinguished himself with his gallantry, he was also wounded. Throughout much of the encampment at Valley Forge, Lafayette served as Washington's right-hand man, going on scouting and foraging parties and helping out whenever and wherever he could.

DECEMBER 1777

As winter approached, General Washington knew he needed a place to camp. He wanted to be close enough to Philadelphia to keep an eye on Howe but far enough away to keep from being caught off guard. On December 19, 1777, he led his troops to a bend along the Schuylkill River near an old ironwork known as Valley Forge. The high ground sloping up from the river made the site easy to defend.

Sergeant John Smith wrote in his diary that on December "the 19th in the morning we marchd to our winter Quarters we marchd all Day without Victuals having nothing to Eat."

Lafayette added, "The army frequently passed whole days without food. The patience and endurance of the soldiers and officers was a miracle."

There are reports that the shoeless soldiers left a trail of blood on their march to Valley Forge. On April 21, Washington wrote to John Banister, "To see men ... without shoes by which their marches might be traced by the blood from their feet ... is a mark of patience and obedience which in my opinion can scare be parallel'd."

On Christmas it snowed four inches and the temperature fell below freezing. That day Washington had planned a surprise attack against a large British foraging unit, but his own food shortages forced him to call off the raid.

The problem was not so much that there was no food. Rather, farmers did not want to accept worthless Continental money that Congress had printed. Some farmers instead sold their crops and animals to the British for gold. The food Washington could get was not always the best. Often, soldiers ate fire cakes, which were made by mixing flour with water and cooking it over hot stones. Fire cakes were not very tasty.

Sometimes, the men simply took food wherever they found it. In his diary Sergeant Smith wrote, "We found a corn field where [there] was corn which we took and ate. After we roasted it in the fire, we pounded [it] with two stones and made some to thicken our broth. We carried [the rest] to [the] mill and got it ground into meal."

JANUARY 1778: BUILDING HUTS

Washington's battle that winter was not against the British. Rather, he and his brave men fought the weather, hunger, and shortages of supplies such as shoes, blankets, tents, and arms.

The winter of 1777–1778 did not have the worst weather of the Revolutionary War. However, even an average Pennsylvania winter can be harsh, especially for people camping outside. Many days were nasty, cold, rainy, and muddy. Washington knew that the first thing his men would need to do was build shelters.

The day before they marched into Valley Forge, Washington divided the army into squads of twelve men and ordered them to build log huts fourteen feet wide and sixteen feet long, with a stone fireplace at one end and a door facing the road at the other end. To encourage his soldiers to work quickly, he offered twelve dollars to the squad in each regiment that finished its "hut in the quickest and most workman-like manner." Within three weeks, most of the soldiers were living in cabins, but some did not complete theirs until February.

While the men were building their huts, Thomas Paine visited Valley Forge. In a letter to Benjamin Franklin, who was in France seeking help, Paine wrote, "They appeared to me like a family of beavers, everyone busy, some carrying logs, others mud, and the rest plastering them together."

The huts did provide a roof over the soldiers' heads, but they were far from comfortable. Twelve soldiers were crowded into these small cabins. There were no windows, so when the soldiers burned wood that was not completely dry, the huts filled with smoke.

Thomas Paine

About this time Tom Paine visited Valley Forge. He had written a pamphlet, *Common Sense*, which strongly cried out for America's independence. It was so popular that George Washington read it and said, "I find *Common Sense* is working a powerful change in the minds of many men."

Paine also wrote another booklet, *The Crisis*. It begins with the stirring words, "These are the times that try men's souls. The summer soldier and sunshine patriot will, in this crisis, shrink from the service of his country." After reading this pamphlet, Washington was so inspired that he ordered his officers to read it to their troops.

JANUARY 1778: HEADQUARTERS

Washington needed a place to meet with officers to plan strategies and to write letters and orders, so he rented a stone house from Deborah Hewes. There he worked tirelessly, organizing his army. He wrote letters to Patrick Henry in Virginia, and to Colonel Alexander Hamilton and Major General Lafayette, who were at Valley Forge. He wrote letters to other officers asking them to find good horses. He even wrote letters to British General Howe, mostly about exchanging prisoners. Washington also sent letter after letter to Congress, begging for supplies. Sometimes he lost his temper when shoes, blankets, clothing, food, and guns did not arrive.

Unfortunately, the Continental Congress had little power to tax the thirteen states. Once, Congress ran a lottery, but even that did not raise much money. And when generous states, such as Connecticut and Massachusetts, sent supplies, getting the goods to Valley Forge was difficult. The wagons had to cross the Hudson and Delaware Rivers, where there were no bridges. Some broke down on the very rough roads or while driving through rivers with rocky bottoms. Colonel Israel Angell wrote in his diary, "There was one Malencully [Melancholy] Accident hapen'd the night before last. Eight waggons & [hors]es and their Drivers was all drownd [crossi]ng Schuylkill."

Alexander Hamilton

Alexander Hamilton was born on an island in the British West Indies in 1755 or 1757. Not long after he arrived in America, he joined a debating club at King's College, now called Columbia University. He was appointed captain of a New York artillery unit and was in one of the boats that crossed the Delaware with Washington when the American army surprised the Hessians in Trenton.

Washington appreciated Hamilton's organizational skills so much that he appointed Hamilton as one of his *aide-de-camps*. In this job, he drafted much of Washington's correspondence. Quick-witted, Hamilton was the life of every party.

He went on to help write the *Federalist Papers* and serve as Washington's secretary of the treasury. He also helped Washington write his farewell address.

In 1804 he was killed in a duel with Aaron Burr, his political rival.

JANUARY 1778: THE ARMY

By January 1778 Washington's army was in poor condition. Of 12,000 men, a little more than half were fit for duty. Sadly, 1,800 died of disease that winter. The soldiers were mostly young, between eighteen and twenty-four. Even the officers were young: Lafayette was only twenty years old, and Alexander Hamilton was twenty-two.

The men came from all walks of life. There were carpenters, shoemakers, blacksmiths, silversmiths, farmers, masons, rope makers, clerks, bakers, brewers, printers, lawyers, and teachers. There were Scots, Welsh, Irish, English, Germans, Portuguese, Jewish Americans, and free African Americans. A black soldier from Connecticut named Jethro was one of the first soldiers to give his life for his country at Valley Forge. One Rhode Island regiment was made up mostly of blacks who were said to be strong, robust men, sturdy and able-bodied. There were also Native Americans. One morning a French soldier was out walking when he heard someone singing a French opera. He was surprised to discover that the singer was a Native American who could speak French and English. It turned out that the soldier had been raised by Jesuit priests.

Even though the men endured hardships, they did not sit around campfires brooding. The camp was a busy place. Small groups of men went out each day in search of food and clothing. Every day hundreds of men performed guard duty. Civilians came to visit. In the spring new recruits arrived daily to replace departing soldiers who had ended their time of service.

FEBRUARY 1778

Even after the huts were completed, the men suffered in the foul weather. On February 27, 1778, Colonel Angell wrote about his hut.

It begun to Storm Extreem hard & our hutt Leakt So bad that my Bed and Cloathes were Soon all weet. . . . in the morning, our hutt all of a flooat. . . . It Still Continued Raining, till about Noon, when it begun to Snow and Snow'd all the after Noon.

Some squads had dug their huts two feet deep into the ground. On the cold days the earth kept the huts warmer. But when spring came the sunken floors became damp. Unsanitary conditions caused illness. Some men would simply toss bones and scraps on the floor, attracting insects and rats, which spread disease. Therefore, Washington ordered "all bones, putrid meat, dirty straw and any other kind of filth to be every day collected and burnt." He also ordered his officers to inspect the huts.

Under such dreadful conditions, it's no wonder that many officers resigned, and many soldiers deserted camp. When deserters were caught, Washington believed the army should make those men an example to others. Most deserters received fifty lashes and rejoined their units. One deserter was executed.

On the outskirts of the camp lived wives and girlfriends of the soldiers. These women did laundry, mended clothing, and cared for the sick.

George Washington was delighted when his wife, Martha, arrived at Valley Forge on February 10, 1778. She soon turned the Heweses' stone house into a home. Even today, the inside of this house looks cozy and comfortable.

In the evenings the officers and their wives often met at one another's quarters. Since there was little entertainment, anyone who could sing was expected to lead the others in popular songs of the day, such as "A Toast," which was a tribute to Washington, and "Johnny Has Gone for a Soldier."

Johnny Has Gone for a Soldier

Here I sit on But-ter-milk Hill, Who can blame me, cry my fill? And ev-'ry tear would turn a mill; Since John-ny has gone for a sol - dier.

FEBRUARY 1778: CLOTHING

The British soldiers looked sharp in their red coats, white pants, and black leather boots. Many Continental soldiers did not even have shoes, so they wrapped their feet in rags. Some with no coats covered themselves in blankets. Others stayed in their huts while men with warmer clothing performed outdoor duties, such as standing guard.

Surgeon Albigence Waldo wrote in his diary, "There come a soldier. His bare feet are seen through his worn-out shoes—his legs nearly naked from the tattered remains of an only pair of stockings—his Breeches are not sufficient to cover his nakedness—his Shirt hanging in Strings—his hair disheveled—his face meagre."

Clothing was supposed to be supplied by the Continental Congress, but because it had little money, individual states equipped their men. Some state regiments were better off than others. Men from Connecticut seemed to have more and better clothing.

Men wore all kinds of hats, some sporting bucktails and cockades. At Valley Forge, General Anthony Wayne ordered his officers to make their men wear the same hats in a soldierlike position. Nevertheless, many were happy just to have hats and wore whatever was available. Others defiantly wore floppy hats as a sign that even though they were in an army, they were not about to give up their individuality. General Wayne also ordered his men to get haircuts. While haircuts helped the men look neat and trim, he was more concerned with reducing the spread of lice.

Washington spent countless hours trying to find food, clothing, muskets, tents, and horses for his army. Happily, this problem improved when Washington asked Congress to appoint Nathanael Greene as quartermaster general in charge of transportation. Through Greene's skill, much-needed supplies were able to be delivered to the troops.

A Special Occasion

On February 22, 1778, a band at Valley Forge serenaded Washington on his forty-sixth birthday. Colonel Proctor's regiment included one fife major, one drum major, one music master, seven drummers, six fifers, and five other unnamed musicians. In some other Continental bands, musicians also played valveless trumpets, valveless French horns, trombones, and an instrument called a serpent, which looked like a long curly snake that played parts that would be played by today's tuba. We may assume that musicians playing these instruments performed for Washington on his special day.

MARCH 1778: CONDITIONS

Keeping clean at Valley Forge was not easy. There was no hot running water. There were no showers, and not much soap. People did not even know to wash their hands before preparing food or eating. At that time, some people believed that it was unhealthy to be in water for any length of time. Washington said that "the custom of remaining long in the water is to be discontinued, as it is far too relaxing and injurious to health."

To groom their hair, the men would sprinkle flour on their heads, which attracted lice. Since lice carry disease, more men became sick.

Sick and wounded soldiers were cared for in hospitals in Trenton, New Jersey, and in Pennsylvania—in Reading, in Bethlehem; at the Cloisters, a religious community in Ephrata; and by the Moravians in Lititz. Traveling to faraway hospitals, sick and wounded men had to ride in carts and wagons over bumpy, rutted roads.

The men suffered from typhoid fever, also known as putrid fever; pneumonia; dysentery; and smallpox. William Brown, a physician and surgeon, said it was "the opinion of every prescribing physician and surgeon, as well as my own, that a large proportion of the men that have died in the hospital the last campaign would probably have been saved, had they enjoyed the advantages of suitable provisions, the means of cleanliness, and medicines."

To keep smallpox from spreading, Washington ordered all troops to be inoculated. In those days there were no syringes, so physicians drew a fine sewing needle into the skin of a sick soldier and then drew that needle under the skin of a well soldier. This would make the well soldier sick for a short while, but kept him from coming down with dreaded smallpox.

MARCH, APRIL, AND MAY 1778

Washington knew how to find the right men for the right jobs. He knew he had to deal with a lack of order and discipline. But he had little time to train the men. On February 23 a volunteer from Prussia (now part of Germany), Baron Wilhelm Augustus von Steuben, reported to Valley Forge. Washington realized that he was the perfect officer to get the troops in shape.

When Baron von Steuben set out to turn the Continental troops into a professional army, he decided to teach by example. So, instead of drilling the entire army at once, he was given an expanded commander in chief's guard to serve as a model. He taught these men the basics—standing straight, keeping heads up, with arms hanging to their sides. He taught them to face right and left, to march in files, and while marching in files, to turn.

Von Steuben soon learned that Americans were unlike European troops. Americans did not automatically follow orders as European troops did. Von Steuben found that he needed to explain the reasons for his commands to these independent-minded soldiers. Though von Steuben spoke very little English, he could speak French. So, he wrote out his regulations in French, and then his aide, Duponceau, translated them into English. When the troops performed well, von Steuben would smile and say "*Gut*" (good) or "*Wunderbar*" (wonderful). But when they made mistakes, he swore at them in German and French. Once, he became so angry that he turned to his aide and told him, "Swear for me in English!"

Alexander Hamilton then helped to rewrite these military drills and rules, titled *Regulations for the Order and Discipline of the Troops of the United States,* which became known simply as the Blue Book. Von Steuben realized that threats and punishments would not unite his troops. While the British flogged soldiers who did not follow orders, von Steuben instead created a bond of loyalty among his men.

So, von Steuben drilled this model company. Then they demonstrated to the rest of the troops how to march and load their muskets by orders. Most infantry soldiers carried muskets, which were called firelocks because when shot, they spit out a flash of fire. That is where we get the term *firearms* for small weapons such as pistols and revolvers. These muskets could fire only one shot before they had to be reloaded. The quickest way to reload together was on command.

First, a soldier pulled back the cock, the part that holds the flint, into the half-cocked position. (That's where we get the phrase "going off half-cocked.")

The next order was "Handle your cartridge." The soldier grabbed a cartridge out of his box, bit off the twist of paper, and poured the powder into the musket. Black powder and smoke from fired rounds would be smeared onto his mouth and face.

One could easily tell from their faces which soldiers had been in battle.

Then the officer ordered, "Draw your rammers," and the soldiers removed the rammer attached to the musket barrel.

"Ram down your charge." Soldiers rammed the cartridge down the barrel.

"Return your rammer." Soldiers put the rammer back onto the barrel.

"Shoulder your firelocks."

"Poise your firelocks."

"Cock your firelocks."

"Fire!"

The order "Aim" was not given because the muskets were not accurate. The muskets could not shoot very straight or very far. Shots traveled only about eighty to one hundred yards. The best chance of hitting a target with a musket was for a line of soldiers to fire a volley of shots all together.

British soldiers were experts at charging the enemy with fixed bayonets. Up until this time, the Americans did not fight this way very well. Von Steuben soon taught them how to attack with fixed bayonets.

With rows of men firing muskets and cannon booming, a battle became so noisy that soldiers could not hear orders from their officers. So, orders were sent to the soldiers by means of fifes and drums. The high-pitched fife and crisp drumbeats could be heard over the din of battle. The commander instructed the fifes and drums to sound orders to advance, wheel, or retreat.

Fife and drum corps also played for other occasions. Each company had one fifer and one drummer. Each regiment had a fife major and a drum major. Their music awakened the men in the morning or called the men to assemble. To accompany the fifes, the drummers beat the proper rhythm for funeral marches, parading, or marching off to battle.

Because von Steuben was drilling his troops to drumbeats, drummers practicing nearby confused von Steuben's company. Therefore, Washington forbade drummers from playing except between five and six in the morning and four and five in the afternoon. He ordered that "drummers that shall be found practicing at any other time . . . shall be severely punished!"

MAY 1778

Washington knew he needed to stay in constant touch with his officers and discuss orders with them. So, every day he had dinner with some of his officers and asked them for their comments on major matters.

Writing about Washington in his journal, Samuel Downing, a private from New Hampshire, said, "We love him."

But not everyone believed Washington should be commander in chief. A few officers, led by General Thomas Conway, believed that Horatio Gates, the general who defeated the British at Saratoga, should be commander in chief. They maneuvered to replace Washington.

At one time Lafayette was a friend of Conway. But when he and many of the troops learned of Conway's plan, known as the Conway Cabal, Lafayette and the officers rallied behind their general with cries of "Washington or no army!" Soon afterward, Conway resigned from the army and the whole matter disappeared.

Washington also enjoyed throwing and catching a ball with his officers. When spring came, the men played a game called base, an early form of baseball. On May 4, Washington dined with his artillery commander, General Henry Knox. Afterward, Washington played wicket, a form of cricket, a British game like baseball. Wicket was played with a long, shovel-shaped bat that was straight on one side and spoon-shaped on the other. A player in the field would roll a ball to a wicket, which was like a simple goalpost. When the batter guarding the wicket hit the ball, he had to run to the base of the one who bowled the ball and then return to the wicket. The soldiers also played another game called shinny, which was similar to what we know as field hockey.

Washington enjoyed watching his officers perform the play *Cato* by Joseph Addison, which is about a Roman statesman who was brave enough to stand up to Caesar. Washington was so fond of this play that he even included a few lines from it in his own farewell address.

On February 6, 1778, France became an ally of the United States. However, this news did not reach Valley Forge until April 30. On May 6, Washington ordered a celebration, a *feu de joie*, which means "joyful fire" in French. Thirteen cannon, one for each of the thirteen states, boomed shots, followed by soldiers firing blank cartridges.

One officer wrote in his diary, "There was a universal clap, with loud huzzas, which continued till he [Washington] had proceeded a quarter of a mile, during which time there were a thousand hats tossed in the air. His Excellency [Washington] turned round with his retinue and huzzaed several times."

JUNE 1778

Why did Washington's men put up with the lack of food and clothing, the cold, wet weather and damp huts? Many felt a duty to the patriotic cause. Many felt loyalty to their fellow soldiers. And as the troops became convinced that the public was not fully supporting them, they came to believe that the only way to win independence was to fight together as one army under the command of Washington.

Few men could have done what Washington did that winter. He took a defeated army in need of almost everything and helped them become a strong fighting force. He did this by listening to others, controlling his own temper, and getting others to stop squabbling. He took men from eleven different states (Georgia and South Carolina did not have troops at Valley Forge) with different ways of doing things and brought them together to become one army with one goal—Liberty. By the time they broke camp, his troops believed that man for man they were just as good as the professional British and Hessian soldiers.

On June 18, 1778, Washington led his army out of Valley Forge and off to battle at Monmouth, New Jersey. Sitting on their horses, Lafayette, von Steuben, and other generals watched the troops parade past. Soldiers cheered the generals and sang songs such as "Yankee Doodle." Surviving the winter at Valley Forge gave the Continental army confidence that they could win independence. On October 19, 1781, they succeeded when General Cornwallis surrendered his army to General Washington at Yorktown, Virginia.

Today, Valley Forge is a national park covering more than 3,468 acres. Strolling the grounds, you will find a visitor's center, a chapel, the National Memorial Arch, reconstructed soldiers' huts, rows and rows of cannon, and monuments. People jog, walk, and ride horses through the park. In warm weather families picnic on the grassy hills that look just as they did when Washington and his army camped there during the winter of 1777 and 1778.

BIBLIOGRAPHY

Alderfer, E. G. *The Ephrata Commune: An Early American Counterculture.* Pittsburgh: University of Pittsburgh Press, 1985.

Babits, Lawrence E. *A Devil of a Whipping: The Battle of Cowpens.* Chapel Hill, N.C.: University of North Carolina Press, 1998.

Bill, Alfred Hoyt. *Valley Forge: The Making of an Army.* New York: Harper, 1952.

Blumenthal, Walter Hart. *Women Camp Followers of the American Revolution.* Philadelphia: George S. MacManus, 1952.

Bober, Natalie S. *Countdown to Independence.* New York: Atheneum, 2001.

Bodle, Wayne. *The Valley Forge Winter: Civilians and Soldiers at War.* University Park, Penn.: The Pennsylvania State University Press, 2002.

Boyle, Lee J. "The Israel Angell Diary," *Rhode Island History.* Vol. 58, no. 1 (November 2000): 106–138.

Brenner, Barbara. *If You Were There in 1776.* New York: Bradbury, 1994.

Brookhiser, Richard. *Founding Father. Rediscovering George Washington.* New York: The Free Press, 1996.

———. *Rules of Civility: The 110 Precepts That Guided Our First President in War and Peace.* New York: The Free Press, 1997.

———. *Alexander Hamilton: American.* New York: The Free Press, 1999.

Camus, Raoul F. *Military Music of the American Revolution.* Chapel Hill, N.C.: University of North Carolina Press, 1976.

Clark, Harrison. *All Cloudless Glory: The Life of George Washington from Youth to Yorktown.* Vol. 1. Washington: Regnery, 1995.

Crane, Elaine Forman, ed. *The Diary of Elizabeth Drinker.* Vol. 1. Boston: Northeastern University Press, 1991.

Flexner, James Thomas. *Washington: The Indispensable Man.* Boston: Little, Brown, 1974.

Fritz, Jean. *Where Was Patrick Henry on the 29th of May?* New York: Coward, McCann & Geoghegan, 1975.

———. *Why Not, Lafayette?* New York: Putnam, 1999.

Jackson, John W. *Valley Forge: Pinnacle of Courage.* Gettysburg, Penn.: Thomas, 1992.

Ledbetter, Bonnie S. "Sports and Games of the American Revolution." *Journal of Sport History.* Vol. 6, no. 3 (winter 1979): 29–40.

Ludlum, David, M. *The Weather Factor.* Boston: Houghton Mifflin, 1984.

Marrin, Albert. *The War for Independence: The Story of the American Revolution.* New York: Atheneum, 1988.

———. *George Washington and the Founding of a Nation.* New York: Dutton, 2001.

Meltzer, Milton. *George Washington and the Birth of Our Nation.* New York: Watts, 1986.

Middlekauff, Robert. "Why Men Fought in the American Revolution." *Continental Army.* Vol. 43, no. 2 (spring 1980): 135–148.

Morris, Richard B. *The American Revolution.* Minneapolis: Lerner, 1985.

Reed, John F. *Campaign to Valley Forge.* Philadelphia: University of Pennsylvania Press, 1965.

Royster, Charles. *A Revolutionary People at War: The Continental Army & American Character. 1775–1783.* Chapel Hill, N.C.: University of North Carolina Press, 1979.

Scheer, George F., and Hugh F. Rankin. *Rebels & Redcoats: The American Revolution Through the Eyes of Those Who Fought and Lived It.* New York: Da Capo, 1957.

Silber, Irwin, ed. *Songs of Independence.* Harrisburg, Penn.: Stackpole Books, 1973.

Spicatto, S. G. "18th Century Military Bands." *The Drummer's Call.* Vol. 5, no. 1 (summer 1993): 25.

Trussell, John B. B., Jr. *Birthplace of an Army.* Harrisburg, Penn.: Pennsylvania Historical and Museum Commission, 1998.

Washington, George. *Orderly Book of General George Washington, Commander-in-chief of the American Armies, Kept at Valley Forge 18 May–11 June, 1778.* Boston: Lamson, Wolffe and Company, 1898.

———. *George-isms.* New York: Atheneum, 2000.

Wright, Mike. *What They Didn't Teach You About the American Revolution.* Novato, Calif.: Presido, 1999.

Zlatich, Marko. *General Washington's Army I: 1775–1778.* London: Osprey, 1994.

PRIMARY SOURCES

Brown, William. *Papers of the Continental Congress, 1774–1789,* Lititz. To Medical Com. 20 January 1778. 6 p. M2247, r91 i78, v2, p. 368.

Smith, John. *The John Smith Diary.* Miss. Dept., Octavo Vol. "S". Worcester, Mass.: American Antiquarian Society, n.d.

Waldo, Albigence. "Valley Forge: Diary of Surgeon Albigence Waldo of the Connecticut Line." *The Pennsylvania Magazine of History and Biography.* Vol. XXI, 1897. Philadelphia: The Historical Society of Pennsylvania, n.d.

Washington, George. "General Orders, April 10, 1778." George Washington Papers at the Library of Congress. Available from http://memory.loc.gov/ammen/gwhtml/gwhome.html; INTERNET.

Washington, George. "Letter to John Banister, April 21, 1778." George Washington Papers at the Library of Congress. Available from http://memory.loc.gov/ammen/gwhtml/gwhome.html; INTERNET.

Washington, George. "General Orders, August 17, 1779." George Washington Papers at the Library of Congress. Available from http://memory.loc.gov/ammen/gwhtml/gwhome.html; INTERNET.

NOTES

References are to sources cited in the bibliography.

Page

3   "Give me Liberty or Give me Death": quoted in Bober, p. 241

3   "He rode . . . power": quoted in Brookhiser, 1999, p. 111

6   "Shake not . . . other": quoted from Washington, 2000, p. 14

6   "Mock not . . . biting": quoted from Washington, 2000, p. 39

6   "Speak not . . . unjust": quoted from Washington, 2000, p. 69

10   "the 19th . . . Eat": quoted from Smith, unpaged

10   "the army . . . miracle": quoted in Jackson, p. 63

10   "To see men . . . parallel'd": quoted from Washington, "Letter to John Banister"

10   "We found corn . . . meal": quoted from Smith. unpaged

12   "hut in the . . . manner": quoted in Jackson, p. 174

12   "They appeared . . . together": quoted in Trussell, p. 18

12   "I find . . . men": quoted in Wright, p. 104

12   "These are . . . country": quoted in Wright, p. 104

14   "There was one . . . Schuylkill": quoted in Boyle, p. 131

18   "It begun . . . Noon": quoted in Boyle, p. 130–131

18   "all bones . . . burnt": quoted from Washington, "General Orders, April 10, 1778"

20   "There come . . . meagre": quoted from Waldo, p. 307

22   "Custom . . . health": quoted from Washington, "General Orders, August 17, 1779"

22   "the opinion . . . medicines": quoted in Brown, p. 368

24   "Swear for . . . English": quoted in Scheer and Rankin, p. 308

26   "drummers that . . . punished": quoted in Jackson, p. 177

28   "We love him": quoted in Jackson, p. 45

28   "There was . . . times": quoted in Scheer and Rankin, p. 317